Megan & Jordan McFall

Picking Up the Pieces

An Advent Study

Picking Up the Pieces

AN ADVENT STUDY

MEGAN & JORDAN MCFALL

INTRODUCTION

Advent is a season within the church during which we celebrate the hope, joy, peace and love in Jesus. Advent at its heart also is a season of waiting. The word "Advent," in its Latin origin, means "coming." The church waits for the coming of Christ. Genesis tells us that before the creation of the universe, chaos reigned. Our Creator God dispersed the chaos, speaking substance and order into nothingness. God, in the simple beauty of a word, set the universe spinning, wrapped in perfection.

Have you ever received a perfectly wrapped gift? The edges are pristinely creased, and the bow and ribbon are in complete symmetrical alignment. Your fingers hover over the immaculate creation, reluctant to tear into such a masterfully adorned package. How could you mar such a skillfully crafted masterpiece? Though this analogy is a dim reflection of God's absolute perfection, a present like this can help remind us of God's work in creation.

But we know the rest of the story, don't we? We barely tasted God's ideal before we turned the world upside down. We treated creation like a present to be opened, used, abused, and discarded, when the true gift of relationship with the most high God was right in front of us. This sin, as we call it, reversed the order of creation. The fall of Adam and Eve brought brokenness into every life that would be birthed onto this newly off-kilter planet, and chaos reigned once again.

As a result of corrupting creation, the people of God embarked on a journey of repentance and atonement, but no matter what they did or how many sacrifices they offered, they could not restore order. Only God could bring life back into perfect alignment. God began to whisper promises of realignment through prophets, and hope was birthed again in the nation of Israel. God whispered through Isaiah, permeating the darkness: "The people who have walked in the darkness have seen a great light." Advent: A longing for something more, for order to be restored, for brokenness to be redeemed. And so the lungs of the Christ child opened to the earth's air as He took his first human breath over two thousand years ago. With Christ's first breath, the chaos began to dissolve once again, darkness dissipated, introducing hope, joy, peace, and love into the longing and desperately broken creation.

While tastes of joy, hope, and order have been re-introduced to the world through Christ, there is still something inside of us that is aching, longing for more. While we can experience pieces of God's hope, joy, love, and peace, we also look around us both witnessing and experiencing painful contrasts to this beauty. Sin, brokenness, despair, sadness, and chaos still flood the earth, causing us to feel desperate and helpless against the darkness.

Instead of looking with admiration at the perfect gift, we feel more like we are shaking our heads in dismay as we examine the disheveled aftermath of Christmas morning. Wrapping paper is torn to shreds and scattered across the floor along with all of our unspoken unmet expectations; we are a mess.

This catastrophe leaves us longing for more, something we can't quite put into words, but we feel all the same. We long for the fulfillment of these things that we so often talk about. We talk about hope, joy, peace, and love at Christmas, so why do we still feel so bereft of the abundance of these promises in our daily existence?

Why do our hearts ache with unfulfilled desires and hopes? Why do we suffer and watch those we love suffer? Why do we bear the excruciating marks of the screaming brokenness that was launched into existence back in the garden?

All of our questions lead us to part of the reality of what is often called the already-but-not-yet of God's Kingdom; the idea that we can have and experience pieces of God's reign and Kingdom here and now, but they are not yet fully here. In those "thin spaces" in life, we catch inklings, glimpses, and rays of hope that manifest the Kingdom of Heaven that touch our awareness every so often. We experience joy and sadness, hope and despair, peace and turmoil, love and hate, and we struggle mightily to make sense of it all.

For some of us, it doesn't feel like there is much hope, joy, peace or love this Advent season. Some of us haven't felt hope, joy, peace, or love for years. This book is for you, for me, and surely for all of us when we get gut-level honest with ourselves. It is about waiting for and living into the fullness of the hope, peace, joy and love that comes in Jesus.

It is our hope that through this book we may begin to allow God to pick up the pieces of our lives so that as Christmas morning draws near we may all the more experience the Kingdom of God on earth as it is in heaven.

As we journey through Advent together, our prayer is that we might experience the richness and abundance of the true hope, joy, peace, and love of Jesus in each of our lives. Emmanuel, God with us, came to bring order into the midst of chaos. Join us as we journey together from chaos to hopeful anticipation as Jesus turns a mess into an amazing miracle.

Guide

Throughout this study you will find each week divided by the themes of hope, joy, peace, and love. Each week we will journey together as we look to reclaiming these things in our lives. Every day you will be invited to spend some time reading and offered the opportunity to reflect upon what you have read. As you prayerfully contemplate individually and in groups, we invite you to either use the reflect section as a guide or follow the Spirit's leading in a different direction. While there is not a specific section each day for responding, our hope is that as you journey through this guide, your time reading and reflecting would move you to responding through prayer, repentance, action, or in other ways as the Holy Spirit leads each day. You will notice that there is not a daily reading each Sunday. We have intentionally designed the study in this way, as we invite you to spend this day gathered with your worshipping community. In addition, at the end of the book you will find guides for four small group sessions. We believe that when we gather together the Holy Spirit will be with us in powerful ways. We encourage you to use these sessions as a guide and to discuss anything from the daily sessions that has impacted you. Our prayer is this study may not only inspire you but also invite you to enter into a deeper walk with Jesus.

In Christ with Love,

Megan and Jordan McFall

HOPE

WEEK 1

MONDAY

Read

"From ages past no one has heard, no ear has perceived, no eye has seen any God besides you, who works for those who wait for him"

Isaiah 64:4

There are those individuals in this world for whom Advent, or waiting, is nothing new. The concept of waiting is a constant in many of our realities. The attitude of urgent anticipation meets some of us each morning with the rising of the sun. In fact, some have spent the entire night (literal or figurative) in desperate longing.

For what are we waiting? Does an answer rise from our lips as quickly as we utter the question, or do we have to dig deep into our walled off hearts to find some area of brokenness? Readily available or hidden the brokenness is there. We all carry burdens, whether we are eager to admit it or not.

In the time of Advent, the marginalized, oppressed, and suffering welcome us into their world of longing and anticipation, hoping against hope for the sun to rise to illuminate their seemingly interminable night of darkness.

We utter the challenge to God that the prophet Isaiah uttered, "Will you keep silent? Oh that you would tear open the heavens to come down!"(Isaiah 64:1).

When we enter into the spirit of Advent waiting, the materially comfortable and well-fed step out of our manufactured contentment for a brief four weeks. We look up to the heavens with hearts as heavy as boulders, begging, throats dry with longing, teeth clenched, fists tight, desperate for the bleak horizon to be broken with a simple ray of hope. We wait for the Son rise to meet our longing eyes.

"Let your face shine on us so that we may be saved." If it does not, we have nothing. We have never wanted and needed anything more than we need You now. Come, Lord Jesus, come!

Reflect

Have you ever experienced a season of waiting in your life? Something you have hoped and longed for? Though different for each of us, we all have areas in our lives where we are longing and crying out to God to break in and bring hope. Spend some time thinking about areas in your life where your hopes, longings and desires seemingly have gone unanswered. Spend some time taking these things to God in prayer.

TUESDAY

Read

"Grace to you and peace from God our Father and the Lord Jesus Christ. I give thanks to my God always for you because of the grace of God that has been given you in Christ Jesus, for in every way you have been enriched in him, in speech and knowledge of every kind— just as the testimony of Christ has been strengthened among you—so that you are not lacking in any spiritual gift as you wait for the revealing of our Lord Jesus Christ. He will also strengthen you to the end, so that you may be blameless on the day of our Lord Jesus Christ. God is faithful; by him you were called into the fellowship of his Son, Jesus Christ our Lord."

1 Corinthians 1:3-9

In the midst of our desperate longing for the coming of the Lord Jesus, we have a charge or a responsibility. As Paul charged the church, we too, with the end of the coming of the Lord in sight, are called to walk faithfully using the spiritual gifts that God has graciously given to us.

Sometimes in the waiting life seems to be on hold like a pause button has been pushed, and we are watching the screen endlessly pulsate waiting to resume the story. We hold to the faulty belief that we can't start really living until our longings are fulfilled—until we land the right job, we find the right person, we start our perfect family, we put down roots in our dream home, we settle into a set of supportive friends. Our lists can be miles long. Whilst God, the author of our hearts, places desires within our hearts for a reason, He also calls us as He did His followers in Corinth. "Do not lack any spiritual gift while you wait."

We are called to be faithful in the waiting.

We are called to be faithful in the waiting. We are called to be obedient when it is the last thing that we want to do, when we are questioning if God will ever even show up, when we are having a hard time believing that God Himself is faithful. We are still called to be faithful, to press the play button and keep living, keep trusting, and keep walking in righteousness.

The waiting time is precious and irreplaceable. It is a time of growth, ripe with opportunities for God to strengthen our faith muscles. In the fullness of time, when God's promises are made complete, we can look back in a spirit of gratitude knowing that our time of waiting was not wasted.

Paul says to the Corinthians, "God is faithful, who has called you into fellowship with His Son, Jesus Christ." We are to emulate our God as we fellowship with His Son. We trust that God is faithful, and we can be faithful in the time of limbo.

We stand in obedience, believing that in the waiting, God continues to give God's presence. The sweetness of waiting is that it compels us to cling to Jesus like we never have before. As a result, we experience His goodness, sweetness, kindness, and gentleness like we never have before. Hold tight, friends. He who promised is faithful, and He shall keep you until completion.

Reflect

What does it mean for you to be faithful in waiting during this season of your life? How can you faithfully serve using the gifts God has given to you through the power of the Holy Spirit here and now? Don't wait - go do it!

WEDNESDAY

Read

"But in those days, after that suffering, the sun will be darkened, and the moon will not give its light, and the stars will be falling from heaven, and the powers in the heavens will be shaken. Then they will see 'the Son of Man coming in clouds' with great power and glory. Then he will send out the angels, and gather his elect from the four winds, from the ends of the earth to the ends of heaven. From the fig tree learn its lesson: as soon as its branch becomes tender and puts forth its leaves, you know that summer is near. So also, when you see these things taking place, you know that he is near, at the very gates. Truly I tell you, this generation will not pass away until all these things have taken place. Heaven and earth will pass away, but my words will not pass away But about that day or hour no one knows, neither the angels in heaven, nor the Son, but only the Father. Beware, keep alert; for you do not know when the time will come. It is like a man going on a journey, when he

leaves home and puts his slaves in charge, each with his work, and commands the doorkeeper to be on the watch. Therefore, keep awake—for you do not know when the master of the house will come, in the evening, or at midnight, or at cockcrow, or at dawn, or else he may find you asleep when he comes suddenly. And what I say to you I say to all: Keep awake."

Mark 13:24-37

Be alert!

Sometimes we get tired of waiting. Our watch night is long, and our eyes grow heavy.

Imagine a night guard keeping watch, longing for morning, so that he can finally stumble down from his station and fall into the deep sleep for which his body is desperately longing.

The difference between the watchman waiting for morning and the Christian called to alertness, however, is that the watchman knows when his shift is scheduled to end. Mark 13 reminds us to, "Keep alert, for you do not know when the time will come." What if you fall asleep when the keeper of the house comes?

Of course, we all need physical sleep, and thankfully, God is not calling us to pull a series of all-nighters until we get to see Him face-to-face. If this were the case, we would find ourselves to be an exhausted, weak, and depleted group of watchers.

Instead of sleepless nights, He is calling us to be alert to the schemes of the enemy, on guard against complacency and spiritual lethargy. We are called to wield the armor of God as outlined in Ephesians 6. We are called to walk this earth with the awareness that our "battle is not against flesh and blood, but against the cosmic powers of this present darkness." (Ephesians 6:12).

If we walk around like our brothers and sisters in Christ are the enemies, then we have fallen asleep. If we walk around fighting battles against our bodies, our families, our churches, and our communities, then we have entered into complacency and lost our focus. If we forget that our money, our time, and our resources are not really ours, but all are on loan to us from the Giver of perfect gifts, we have lost focus.

Stay spiritually awake. Stay alert. The keeper of the house is coming, and we are the watchmen and watchwomen who are called to celebrate and welcome His return.

Oh, brothers and sisters, our celebration will be spectacular!

Reflect

Are there areas in your life where you have fallen into complacency and spiritual lethargy? Have you been fighting any battles against yourself or others that are distracting you from what God is calling you to focus on? Spend time today asking God to help you refocus on where He is calling you.

THURSDAY

Read

"Be still, and know that I am God! I am exalted among the nations, I am exalted in the earth."

Psalm 46:10

What do you do in order to make waiting more tolerable? We each have a remarkable supply of tactics that we employ to survive times of waiting. Humans operate on a spectrum of "distress tolerance." For most of us, waiting leads to distress. I don't know about you, but I certainly do not enjoy being in distress. As a result of our discomfort in waiting, we employ methods to lessen our distress. They may look like coping mechanisms, habits, hobbies, or even addictions or dysfunctions.

We are excellent at distracting ourselves. Sometimes we take it to the next level: we become masters of denial, convincing ourselves that we really aren't even waiting for anything: that this life in which we are currently existing is the one that is the best possible life for us. If we are not in full-blown denial, we are masters at distracting by staying busy, by engaging in addictive behavior, by filling our lives with so much stuff that there is no room for those things that our heart is desperately craving.

Despite our best-intentioned strategies we still long. In those quiet spaces of the night, in those little cracks in our lives when we stop to catch a breath, in those thin places where heaven brushes earth just a little bit more concretely. In our grief, in our humanness, in our offenses, when we let our defenses fall we catch that glimmer of longing. We cringe at our unmet hopes colliding with our deepest fears.

Friends, in these thin spaces of longing we can come face-to-face with true Advent waiting, and here in the pause we can begin to prepare our hearts for the coming of the long-anticipated Christ Child.

> Advent, if we allow it, offers a thin space, yearly, where heaven brushes earth.

Advent, if we allow it, offers a thin space, yearly, where heaven brushes earth; where we come face-to-face with our deepest longings, our unmet needs; our desperate gut-wrenching, infuriating convictions that all is not even close to being made right in this crumbling, flailing world. Advent strikes a chord in our hearts that resonates with the Hebrews as they heart-wrenchingly cried, "O come, o come, Emmanuel."

We have a way of domesticating the prophet Isaiah, or yet, domesticating Christmas in general. We build up distractions with lights, tinsel, and presents. While there is nothing wrong with cheerfully celebrating Christmas, we often try to drown our longing in eggnog and craftily cover it in sparkling ribbons. We are afraid to descend into the awareness that we are hurting and broken.

Let's all courageously step out of our distractions and denial long enough to recognize our longing as we sing the hymns of Advent desire. Let us cry with the Israelites, begging Emmanuel, our only hope, our rescuer, to come and make right the wrongness of our hearts and of our world.

Reflect

As you wait, are you filling your life with distractions or inviting the Holy Spirit to break into the broken places so that you might experience more joy? What areas in your life do you need to cry out to God asking the Spirit to come and restore? Spend time today lifting up these areas to God in prayer.

FRIDAY

For Those Who Wait

Read

"Blessed are the poor in spirit, for theirs is the kingdom of heaven. Blessed are those who mourn, for they will be comforted. Blessed are the meek, for they will inherit the earth. Blessed are those who hunger and thirst for righteousness, for they will be filled. Blessed are the merciful, for they will receive mercy. Blessed are the pure in heart, for they will see God. Blessed are the peacemakers, for they will be called children of God. Blessed are those who are persecuted for righteousness' sake, for theirs is the kingdom of heaven. Blessed are you when people revile you and persecute you and utter all kinds of evil against you falsely on my account. Rejoice and be glad, for your reward is great in heaven, for in the same way they persecuted the prophets who were before you."

Matthew 5:3-12

We all have those holiday seasons that are a little more melancholy than usual (or downright agonizing). We may have had a hard year financially. We may have faced a life-changing diagnosis. We may have lost someone we never imagined having to live without. We may be shell-shocked and reeling from disaster. Many of us have felt assaulted by Christmas at one time or another, like it is a horrific reminder of our lack of cheer and joy.

We even offer a type of Christmas service for those who don't feel particularly "Christmas-ey." It is called the "Blue Christmas" service. It is a Christmas service with a bit of a different feel, where we acknowledge unmet expectations, broken hearts, and deep losses in light of the Christmas season. It's not all that cheerful, and it is a beautifully honest service. Quite possibly, those who resonate with the need for a blue Christmas service have a leg up from the rest of us.

"Blessed are those who mourn, blessed are the meek, blessed are the poor in spirit, blessed are those who hunger and thirst for righteousnes." Blessed are those of us desperate for Jesus to break through this mess that we call normal and turn the kingdom of this world on it's head.

Maybe we are backwards in thinking that the hurting and broken are "not in the Christmas spirit." Maybe they are exactly the ones that Jesus was pointing to in the Sermon on the Mount. Maybe they are the ones that most relate to the Israelites as they were longing for a Savior, Rescuer, and King. Maybe they are the ones who would have actually recognized Him for who He was: The humble King, Immanuel, God with us. Because really, who needs "God with us" except for someone who is desperate, lonely, and longing?

Until we can recognize the reality of our suffering we cannot begin to open up to the possibility of the redemption that Christ offers.

Reflect

Have you ever experienced a Christmas season where you weren't really feeling in the "Christmas spirit"? Perhaps this season you aren't feeling too joyful. In the midst of this, imagine a God who is with you through the sadness, pain, despair, or brokenness.

SATURDAY

The God of Hope

Read

"In the days of King Herod of Judea, there was a priest named Zechariah, who belonged to the priestly order of Abijah. His wife was a descendant of Aaron, and her name was Elizabeth. Both of them were righteous before God, living blamelessly according to all the commandments and regulations of the Lord. But they had no children, because Elizabeth was barren, and both were getting on in years.

Once when he was serving as priest before God and his section was on duty, he was chosen by lot, according to the custom of the priesthood, to enter the sanctuary of the Lord and offer incense. Now at the time of the incense offering, the whole assembly of the people was praying outside. Then there appeared to him an angel of the Lord, standing at the right side of the altar of incense.

When Zechariah saw him, he was terrified; and fear overwhelmed him. But the angel said to him, "Do not be afraid, Zechariah, for your prayer has been heard. Your wife Elizabeth will bear you a son, and you will name him John. You will have joy and gladness, and many will rejoice at his birth, for he will be great in the sight of the Lord. He must never drink wine or strong drink; even before his birth he will be filled with the Holy Spirit. He will turn many of the people of Israel to the Lord their God. With the spirit and power of Elijah he will go before him, to turn the hearts of parents to their children, and the disobedient to the wisdom of the righteous, to make ready a people prepared for the Lord." Zechariah said to the angel, "How will I know that this is so? For I am an old man, and my wife is getting on in years." The angel replied, "I am Gabriel. I stand in the presence of God, and I have been sent to speak to you and to bring you this good news. But now, because you did not believe my words, which will be fulfilled in their time, you will become mute, unable to speak, until the day these things occur."

Meanwhile the people were waiting for Zechariah, and wondered at his delay in the sanctuary. When he did come out, he could not speak to them, and they realized that he had seen a vision in the sanctuary. He kept motioning to them and remained unable to speak. When his time of service was ended, he went to his home.

After those days his wife Elizabeth conceived, and for five months she remained in seclusion. She said, "This is what the Lord has done for me when he looked favorably on me and took away the disgrace I have endured among my people."

Luke 1:5-25

Zechariah and his wife Elizabeth were familiar with unmet desires. In a time where having children was the mark of being blessed, they were childless, even in their righteousness. After years of hope deferred, seemingly fruitless faithfulness, and prayers that appeared to be left hanging in the balance, waiting for the "yes" from Yahweh, they could do nothing but hope for a miracle.

Zechariah's expectant longing was met by an angel of the Lord who declared that finally his prayers were being answered favorably. Finally, according to the angel, Zechariah and Elizabeth would find their "disgrace" replaced by joy and gladness.

Hope: the advent of the Messiah met Zechariah in a place of jaded, darkened doubt, and Zechariah ever-so-slowly lifted his face to encounter the reality of his life-long desire: A child, a lineage-builder, a life-line, and, best yet, the forerunner of the Christ child.

This child that Zechariah and Elizabeth had built their lives dreaming of, hoping for, praying for, pleading and weeping over, and desperately begging God for, was the size of a lentil, and then a papaya, and then a squash, and then a kumquat.

Zechariah's and Elizabeth's hope was becoming real and swelling in Elizabeth's belly, and this hope would point the world to the One who would be the hope of the nations.

> This hope would point the world to the One who would be the hope of the nations.

Do we feel like Zechariah? That our relentless hoping and praying and dreaming has been met with what feels like mocking, echoing, deafening silence? That our prayers will never be answered? That we cringingly, secretly fear that God is actually just a void of hopelessness?

And then one day, as we limp forward in tentative yet trusting faithfulness, we see the actualization of our dreams. God HAS been listening! Our prayers and pleadings and intercessions are not barren, pointless cries echoing into nothingness! God has heard me! With Elizabeth we can cry, "This is what the Lord has done for me!"

Reflect

Has there ever been a time in your life when it has felt as though hope has been deferred? What areas in your life past or present has it felt as if your prayers have fallen into silence? Has God ever answered your prayers when you least expected it, when hope became real? Reflect on the glimmers of hope God has given to you in the past - and may this give you strength and hope for the unknown of the future.

JOY

WEEK 2

MONDAY

God's People Are Comforted

Read

"Comfort, O comfort my people, says your God. Speak tenderly to Jerusalem, and cry to her that she has served her term, that her penalty is paid, that she has received from the Lord's hand double for all her sins. A voice cries out: "In the wilderness prepare the way of the Lord, make straight in the desert a highway for our God. Every valley shall be lifted up, and every mountain and hill be made low; the uneven ground shall become level, and the rough places a plain. Then the glory of the Lord shall be revealed, and all people shall see it together, for the mouth of the Lord has spoken." A voice says, "Cry out!" And I said, "What shall I cry?" All people are grass, their constancy is like the flower of the field. The grass withers, the flower fades, when the breath of the Lord blows upon it; surely the people are grass. The grass withers, the flower fades;

but the word of our God will stand forever. Get you up to a high mountain, O Zion, herald of good tidings; lift up your voice with strength, O Jerusalem, herald of good tidings, lift it up, do not fear; say to the cities of Judah, "Here is your God!" See, the Lord God comes with might, and his arm rules for him; his reward is with him, and his recompense before him. He will feed his flock like a shepherd; he will gather the lambs in his arms, and carry them in his bosom, and gently lead the mother sheep."

Isaiah 40:1-11

"In the wilderness prepare the way of the Lord, make straight in the desert a highway for our God."

That voice that cries out? Do you know to whom that voice belongs? It is the very child that broke the darkness for Zechariah and Elizabeth; the voice of the child who represented hope, that made way for Hope. The voice of hope cried out in the wilderness, "Make way!"

"Make way…Every valley shall be lifted up, and every hill made low, uneven ground made level." All will finally be made right when the glory of the Lord is revealed. Now, prepare the way! Joy rises. It will come to meet us; let us make way for His arrival. Isaiah called this voice the herald of good tidings. Good news!! All will be made right.

God will make low those who are haughty, and He will lift up those who are humble. Are we willing to prepare the way for the Messiah in our hearts? Jesus is the great sifter of the wheat. Will we humble our hearts so that He will lift us up, or will we mock the seemingly eccentric voice of that crazy dude who ate wild locusts and honey, wore sackcloth, and wandered around in the desert? Then, as a result of our haughty arrogance, will we mock, or, even worse, ignore, the voice of the Savior?

Good news!! All will be made right.

Joy is coming. Comfort is on its way. The glory of the Lord is getting ready to be revealed. Will we prepare the way?

Reflect

What areas in your life are you hoping for joy to begin rising? How are you preparing the way for the Messiah to enter into your heart and mind in deeper ways within your life?

TUESDAY

Room In Distress

Read

*"Answer me when I call, O God of my right!
You gave me room when I was in distress. Be
gracious to me, and hear my prayer."*
                                        Psalm 4:1

When the outcome is unknown, where do we turn? When it is unclear whether we will survive the obstacle ahead of us where do our eyes land? Do they land on the obstacle itself, fixed in fear? Do they move from the obstacle to the God of the universe, resting in trust?

Imagine Mary. Her life is in the most severe form of limbo that she has ever experienced or ever dreamed of experiencing. She is pregnant, impossibly pregnant, with...the child of whom? According to the Angel Gabriel, with God's son. Wait a second. How? Who could possibly understand that scenario? Who would ever believe her? Worse case scenario: she will be stoned.

41

Best case: She will live in shame and isolation the rest of her life.

Unless...God is a God who keeps His promises. Mary, sweet, brave, bold, courageous, undaunted Mary, looks up, and sees her Maker, the Maker of her child, and trusts. "Here I am, the servant of the Lord; let it be to me according to your word" (Luke 1:38). Mary sees her belly swelling with this unbelievable, immaculately conceived child, and she chooses to see God rather than the impossibility of her situation. Because Gabriel told her, "Nothing is impossible with God" (Luke 1:37).

As the Psalmist declares, "You gave me room when I was in distress." Mary sits in that room referred to by the Psalmist. In her distress, she leans into the discomfort of her most massive obstacle. That massive obstacle ultimately ends up being her most astounding miracle.

Why does she lean into this discomfort? How can she bear this discomfort? Just as Gabriel promises her, the Lord is with her in her distress (Luke 1:29). Why do you think that Gabriel greeted her with the declaration that the Lord was with her? I suspect Gabriel's greeting had something to do with the reality that in her moment of revelation, Mary desperately needed the reassurance that she was not alone. What do we need the most in our places of uncertainty and unknown? Presence: the safest, most secure presence imaginable.

As God made space for Mary and accompanied the mother of Jesus into her discomfort, she leaned into the Maker of the Universe, believing that joy would meet her in the impossibility of her situation. Nine months later, she held joy in her arms.

Reflect

Have you ever been placed in a seemingly impossible situation? Perhaps one in which it seemed there was no way out or the outcome could not be predicted. Would you have responded differently if you knew God was with you in the midst of it? What does it look like to find joy, even in the midst of difficult circumstances?

WEDNESDAY

The Other Side of Faithfulness

Read

"In the sixth month the angel Gabriel was sent by God to a town in Galilee called Nazareth, to a virgin engaged to a man whose name was Joseph, of the house of David. The virgin's name was Mary. And he came to her and said, "Greetings, favored one! The Lord is with you." But she was much perplexed by his words and pondered what sort of greeting this might be. The angel said to her, "Do not be afraid, Mary, for you have found favor with God. And now, you will conceive in your womb and bear a son, and you will name him Jesus. He will be great, and will be called the Son of the Most High, and the Lord God will give to him the throne of his ancestor David. He will reign over the house of Jacob forever, and of his kingdom there will be no end." Mary said to the angel, "How can this be, since I am a virgin?" The angel said to her, "The Holy Spirit will come

upon you, and the power of the Most High will overshadow you; therefore the child to be born will be holy; he will be called Son of God. And now, your relative Elizabeth in her old age has also conceived a son; and this is the sixth month for her who was said to be barren. For nothing will be impossible with God." Then Mary said, "Here am I, the servant of the Lord; let it be with me according to your word." Then the angel departed from her."

Luke 1:26-38

Steadfast love and faithfulness will meet; righteousness and peace will kiss each other. Faithfulness will spring up from the ground, and righteousness will look down from the sky."

Psalm 85:10-11

What was the fruit of Mary's faithfulness? Have you ever trusted God through a seemingly unbelievably impossible situation only to discover that God was singularly sufficient to accomplish the impossible?

There is no way to appropriately fathom the magnitude of the calling and the promise that was placed on Mary as she carried God's own Son. I imagine Mary somewhere around twenty weeks pregnant with the Savior of the world after her visit with Angel Gabriel. I picture this teenager, in her second trimester, inadvertently rubbing her hands over her slightly protruding belly, to be startled by a slight, nearly imperceptible flutter. "Was that….? Could it be….? Uh-oh, it just got real. There really is a little human in there? Wait? Is it okay to call God's Son human?"

I imagine the rush of excitement, confusion, and the twinge of fear that Mary would encounter as she felt this first flutters of movement of the prenatal Christ child.

Fear and anxiety carry one down dangerous roads. I imagine Mary placing a guard at the threshold of her consciousness to quell the flood of "what if's" as they rushed upon her while she pondered the presence of the Messiah in her womb.

Faithfulness requires focus, commitment, and trust. Righteousness only comes with intentional devotion and directed seeking after the heart of God. While righteousness is given by God, we also are given the choice about whether or not to cooperate with God as He works out His righteousness within us.

> Mary's faithfulness yielded the fruit of perfect love to set foot on the planet.

Mary's faithfulness yielded the fruit of perfect love to set foot on the planet. Her faithfulness collided with the steadfast love of Jesus, which opened up the planet for redemption and reconciliation with the God of the universe. Through the willing womb of Mary, "righteousness and peace kissed each other" (Psalm 85:10).

On the floor of the stable, next to the trough in which the newborn Jesus was placed, Mary's faithfulness was poured out onto the soil of a desperate, dying world. Her willing womb anointed the long- suffering planet with the joy of a cry that marked the first human breaths of God incarnate. Righteousness looked down from the sky and beamed a radiant smile in the shape of Bethlehem's star.

Reflect

In our faithfulness God will speak joy and life into both our hearts and into the hearts of others. What does it look like for you to be faithful with what God has entrusted to you? Are you willing to be faithful no matter the situation?

THURSDAY

The Leap of Joy

Read

"In those days Mary set out and went with haste to a Judean town in the hill country, where she entered the house of Zechariah and greeted Elizabeth. When Elizabeth heard Mary's greeting, the child leaped in her womb. And Elizabeth was filled with the Holy Spirit and exclaimed with a loud cry, "Blessed are you among women, and blessed is the fruit of your womb. And why has this happened to me, that the mother of my Lord comes to me? For as soon as I heard the sound of your greeting, the child in my womb leaped for joy. And blessed is she who believed that there would be a fulfillment of what was spoken to her by the Lord."

Luke 1:39-45

Many years before Pentecost, the Spirit filled Elizabeth with a power that stirred wombs of two women.

Picture Mary walking to Elizabeth's door, about to burst with anticipation over the news that she was about to share with her cousin. Upon Mary's arrival, Elizabeth spoils the surprise that Mary has planned for her. Mary has her whole story scripted out for Elizabeth. She has rehearsed over and over how she will break the news of her pregnancy to her beloved Elizabeth. Her cousin, however, beat Mary to the punch. The child in Elizabeth's womb managed to tell his mother about Jesus before Mary got the chance to get the words "I'm having God's child" out of her quivering lips.

It is hard to imagine the joy that Elizabeth feels with this new influx of Holy Spirit and Holy insider information about the Christ Child. Elizabeth responds to this powerful indwelling of the Spirit with words of encouragement and joy toward Mary. "Blessed are you among women, and blessed is the fruit of your womb" (verse 42). Herein is the blessing of joy.

...and you will be overtaken by joy

Blessed---happy—are you, Mary. And happy is your Child. Here is your joy. Here is the fruit of God's spirit and your faithfulness. Mary, you have believed God when He told you something unbelievably impossible. He will bring His promise to fruition, and you will be overtaken by joy.

When I imagine the greeting of Mary and Elizabeth, I imagine the resonance in their wombs being like that of two pianos in the same room as they resonate with the same note. When two pianos are in the same room, and a pianist strikes a key on one piano, the strings inside the other piano begin to vibrate, producing the very same note. This is called resonance, and this is the picture that I see when I see the two expecting mothers in the same room.

The children in their bellies resonate with the "joy note." Both mothers are blessed with the most absolute, beautiful, heavenly joy that one can imagine. They gaze into one another's eyes, in awe of the work of this God to whom they have entrusted their lives and the lives of their children.

Reflect

Have you ever experienced joy leaping out of your very soul without even realizing or understanding it? It is often in these situations that joy becomes contagious, resonating with others around you. Ask God to overtake you with joy today and watch as others respond back in joy.

FRIDAY

Mary's Song

Read

"And my spirit rejoices in God my Savior, for he has looked with favor on the lowliness of his servant. Surely, from now on all generations will call me blessed; for the Mighty One has done great things for me, and holy is his name. His mercy is for those who fear him from generation to generation. He has shown strength with his arm; he has scattered the proud in the thoughts of their hearts. He has brought down the powerful from their thrones, and lifted up the lowly; he has filled the hungry with good things, and sent the rich away empty. He has helped his servant Israel, in remembrance of his mercy, according to the promise he made to our ancestors, to Abraham and to his descendants forever." And Mary remained with her about three months and

then returned to her home."

Luke 1:47-56

Let's set the stage. Mary and Elizabeth are basking in the glow of their resonating wombs. Elizabeth's unborn baby has just informed his mommy that Mary is housing the Lord of the universe, and they are in a state of heavenly awe. Elizabeth has just blessed Mary and her baby, and has confirmed the word of Gabriel, just in case Mary had any doubt about the origin and destiny of her child.

The Kingdom of God is one of downward mobility.

God inspires this song from within Mary's heart, which encapsulates the inside-out, upside-down kingdom of God. This kingdom of God is one of downward mobility: the lower you go, the higher you are lifted.

Mary's act of magnifying the Lord is an act of humility, lowering herself, and lifting up Yahweh. Mary's act is a reflection of the act of Christ in His incarnation. The God of the universe, robed in majesty, seated in the heavens, puts on mortality. God takes on corruptible flesh, made of dust and decay, and humbles himself, not just to the world, but to the lowest position in the world:

that of an infant in a lower class family. He lowers Himself, and then lowers Himself even lower.

Mary, who is housing the humble Lord, the size of a lentil, in her womb, imitates Christ in her humility. In her "Magnificat" she presents the upside-down kingdom dynamics: the proud and the powerful are brought low. The rich are sent away empty. Those who are too full of themselves to hunger for Christ will never find true joy and contentment. Only the lowly will be lifted up.

To the proud and puffed up, the kingdom of Jesus is appalling. This kingdom is abhorrent to those who are comfortable in their own kingdoms. To those who are filled with the junk food of self-satisfaction, the offer of pure joy and peace seems unnecessary. It seems threatening, even. How can we be filled with good things if we do not come hungry?

To those who hunger, long, suffer, and recognize their need; to the Marys and the Elizabeths, the shepherds, outcasts, and to those bent down, the Savior comes to raise their heads. He comes to stoop down himself, cup their dusty chin in His hands, and gently raise their faces until their eyes meet His eyes: the eyes of perfect lovingkindness, gentleness, peace, and overwhelming joy.

May we be a people who follow the lead of the Servant-king, the Savior who humbled Himself, who "being made in form of God did not consider equality with God something to be grasped, but made Himself nothing, taking on the form of a servant" (Philippians 2:6).

Let us be imitators of the greatest King who ever walked the face of the planet, the one who served and loved, and became obedient to death, even death on the cross. In this imitation of Christ, may we find the complete joy of the fellowship of His resurrection. Let us manifest the downward mobility of the Kingdom of heaven as we humble ourselves to be raised up by the God of the universe.

Reflect

What does it mean for you to humble yourself in order to serve and love others? How might humbling oneself bring about joy and contentment in your life? What does it mean to hunger and thirst after God? Pray and ask God to reveal area(s) in your life where pride has gotten in the way of truly living into the joy-filled life offered in Jesus.

SATURDAY

The Path to Joy

Read

"For his anger is but for a moment; his favor is for a lifetime. Weeping may linger for the night, but joy comes with the morning."
Psalm 30:5

"May those who sow in tears reap with shouts of joy."
Psalm 126:5

"But there will be no gloom for those who were in anguish. In the former time he brought into contempt the land of Zebulun and the land of Naphtali, but in the latter time he will make glorious the way of the sea, the land beyond the Jordan, Galilee of the nations. The people who walked in darkness have seen a great light; those who lived in a land of deep darkness—on them light has shined."
Isaiah 9:1-2

As we study scriptures on joy, it seems that joy is rather hard-won. Joy seems to ride on the first signs of dawn after the agony of long nights of weeping. It seems to tiptoe into pain-wrought rooms filled with the cold dampness brought on by tears of sorrow. It seems to settle into the bones that are weary and brittle after writhing in pain an anguish. It seems to ride in on the first rays of light as they begin to pierce our years of deep darkness.

Does great joy always require deep suffering? Does beautiful rejoicing have to be preceded by ugly-faced weeping? I'm not sure what the answer is to that question, but I do know this: If we are completely honest with ourselves many of us have experienced, if not are experiencing, excruciating pain. If we have not, we may either be under three months of age, or we may need to evaluate what numbing mechanisms we are relying on in our lives.

Pain is not the enemy. Suffering has never been the enemy. In fact, pain and suffering can be passageways to overwhelming joy.

Have you ever experienced dark seasons of the soul? Where there seems to be no end to the agony? Where loneliness and darkness seem to threaten to consume you? I am confident that I am not alone when I say with conviction that I certainly have!

Friends, those tunnels that seem the darkest, where we wonder if we will ever lay eyes on that proverbial light at the end, are often the most pivotal, formative points in our lives. If we just keep relying on God's grace to help us to place one foot in front of the other, we will emerge on the other side, whether that other side is in this world or the world to come. However you slice it, joy is on the other end!

The good news is this: The people walking in darkness have seen a great light!

The people walking in darkness; those with great burdens; those for whom weeping has become a lifestyle; those who feel like their tears could water all of the yards in the state of Kansas in the middle of drought season; those people: They see the light. It has come, and God has chosen the broken, hurting, longing, weeping, malnourished souls to reveal it to.

Are we willing to come far enough to the end of ourselves to approach the sorrow that leads to joy? We don't have to search for sorrow. It's not too far away. Let us put on hearts that are willing to weep with those who weep, willing to see the reality of our need, willing to face the hurts that we have been trying to bury.

Let us take those broken hearts to the hands of the Savior, who promises beauty in exchange for our ashes, redemption in exchange for our mess, and joy in exchange for our sorrow. This is our

King, our suffering Savior, our wounded Healer. Come, in your hunger, and taste His goodness.

Reflect

Are there hurts or sorrows in your life you have for too long been trying to ignore or bury? Are you willing to open your heart up to experiencing sorrow, whether it be your own or alongside of another? When we truly allow ourselves to feel sorrow, the Holy Spirit in those moments can break in, bringing healing and in turn joy.

PEACE

———

WEEK 3

MONDAY

Rebuilding Ancient Ruins

Read

"The spirit of the Lord God is upon me, because the Lord has anointed me; he has sent me to bring good news to the oppressed, to bind up the brokenhearted, to proclaim liberty to the captives, and release to the prisoners; to proclaim the year of the Lord's favor, and the day of vengeance of our God; to comfort all who mourn; to provide for those who mourn in Zion— to give them a garland instead of ashes, the oil of gladness instead of mourning, the mantle of praise instead of a faint spirit. They will be called oaks of righteousness, the planting of the Lord, to display his glory. They shall build up the ancient ruins, they shall raise up the former devastations; they shall repair the ruined cities, the devastations of many generations."

Isaiah 61:1-4

When Jesus entered into the scene of humanity, He knew that no one could see actual real peace unless the existing social order or injustice and oppression was destroyed. Once the order was done away with, God was free to rebuild the ancient ruins.

The good news of the upside-down gospel of Jesus is that the peace the new order will bring is a kind of peace far greater than the world has ever known. This is a kind of peace that much of the world doesn't even know to hope for because it has never tasted such profound and life-changing peace.

Have you ever felt a kind of longing that seems almost unidentifiable? A longing for something that you can't quite place your finger upon, possibly because though you were created for it, you have never truly experienced the object of this obscure longing? C. S. Lewis, in his argument for Christ in Mere Christianity, identifies this longing as evidence of the existence of God.[1] We are born with an innate desire for goodness, for the wrongs of the world to be made right, and for peace to be restored. In essence, we have the ability to see the chaos of a marred creation and long for wholeness and peace to reign. From where does that longing arise? From the image of God that is imprinted into our very beings.

---

1   Lewis, C.S. Mere Christianity. MacMallin Publishing Co. 1952. New York.

Why would King Herod have been so terrified of this Christ child? Why would he have gone to such extremes to have Him eliminated? Possibly because he knew that his existing order would have to be overthrown in order for the "former devastations" to be built up. He, like every other image-bearer of God on the face of the planet, knew that all was not right in the world.

If this Messiah, the coming King, were to rule in peace, many oppressed peoples must be set free, and his oppressive regime would have to be reversed. Why would he lie to the wise men saying that he wanted to bow down and worship the Christ child in order to get inside information about his whereabouts? Why would he wipe out every boy under the age of two, creating an astronomical slaughter of innocent children? Because he too knew the predictions of the ancient prophets; because his personal peace came at a monstrous cost with outlandish oppression. In order to secure his rule, he placed Judea under constant bondage, casting a canopy of fear and chaos over the Jews.

Peace. The prophet Isaiah promises peace for the oppressed, brokenhearted, and those in bondage. This day of peace that Isaiah promises, through the power of the Spirit, will come at a cost. In order for peace to reign, vengeance must be revealed for the oppressors. Those who bear down on the innocent, who oppress the weak, are the ones who tremble at the promise of peace. They thrive on chaos and fear.

Those who serve the innocent, who raise up and heal the broken, they are the ones who are the peace-lovers. Blessed are the peace-makers, for theirs shall be the kingdom of heaven.

Reflect

Have you ever experienced a great amount of peace in your life? How did you feel when you experienced that peace? Now imagine a peace that is far greater than that. Imagine what the world would look like if it experienced a peace of that magnitude. Deep down, we all long for that peace. What does it mean for you to be a peace-maker within your sphere of influence?

TUESDAY

Read

"For I the Lord love justice, I hate robbery and wrongdoing; I will faithfully give them their recompense, and I will make an everlasting covenant with them. Their descendants shall be known among the nations, and their offspring among the peoples; all who see them shall acknowledge that they are a people whom the Lord has blessed. I will greatly rejoice in the Lord, my whole being shall exult in my God; for he has clothed me with the garments of salvation, he has covered me with the robe of righteousness, as a bridegroom decks himself with a garland, and as a bride adorns herself with her jewels. For as the earth brings forth its shoots, and as a garden causes what is sown in it to spring up, so the Lord God will cause righteousness and praise to spring up before all the nations."

Isaiah 61:8-11

We serve a God who, in His very nature is justice, and therefore abhors injustice. God is freedom and abundance and therefore despises oppression. God, who raises up the weak and lifts up the downcast, speaks vehemently against the strong attacking the weak.

The prophet Isaiah speaks of "shalom", or peace, throughout his prophecy of the Messiah, the "Prince of Peace." This shalom, indicative of a harmonious and symbiotic relationship among all parties, offers hope to the oppressed, and in Isaiah's particular case, the Hebrew nation represents the oppressed and restricted.

The Israelites' situation is one of anything but peace. They find themselves in turmoil, constant fear, oppression, and confusion. They feel an agonizing longing for a safe-haven, somewhere to rest and feel confident that they will not be harmed. They long to take that deep breath of security, where they can let their guards down and finally rest.

The promise of peace probably seems somewhat hollow, given their current state of affairs. And yet God through His spokespersons has communicated a foreshadowing of the shalom of which they have only dreamed.

This peace, which ultimately produces the fruit of righteousness, namely, a right relationship between God and man, is not a distant ideal. It is not an impossibility that could never be accomplished.

> This peace, which ultimately produces the fruit of righteousness, namely, a right relationship between God and man, is not a distant ideal.

God does not create us with innate longings for justice, peace, and righteousness without ultimately promising to deliver on His promises. Jesus Christ brings it to earth as a reality, in the current order, and in the heavenly order. He comes to lift up the oppressed, and He comes to bring rightness of relationship between the offender and the offended. Jesus comes to restore relationships, between God and the beloved humanity, between nations and peoples, and even our relationships with ourselves. Where we are broken and divided, Jesus comes to bring unity and wholeness. There is no end to the mending that Jesus can provide to willing, yielded hearts. Will we let Him heal us?

Reflect

Where have you experienced or seen injustice and oppression in your life? What would it look like for God to speak His peace into those situations? To see broken relationships in your life, with God, family or friends restored by the Grace of God? Perhaps God is calling you to step out in faith to look at restoring a broken relationship in your life.

WEDNESDAY

Restored to Relationship

Read

> *"May the God of peace himself sanctify you entirely; and may your spirit and soul and body be kept sound and blameless at the coming of our Lord Jesus Christ. The one who calls you is faithful, and he will do this."*
> *1 Thessalonians 5:23-24*

The prophet Isaiah foretold of the coming of the "Prince of Peace". Some of us might interpret this title given to Jesus to mean that He will restore world peace.

What is one of the most common themes at Christmas time? What is the reoccurring them in Christmas carols, secular and sacred? What was always on Amy Grant's "Grown up Christmas List"?[1] Peace on earth.

---

1   Linda Thompson & David Foster. 1992

We picture a happy, cheerful, well-adjusted earth in unity with a big red Christmas bow tied around it. While this is an appropriate picture of the Kingdom of our Lord which is to come, this is only part of what we understand shalom to offer.

Our Prince of Peace entered the world not only to make right our relationships with one another, nation-to-nation, ruler-to-ruler, oppressor-to oppressed. This Prince of peace is the one who came to restore us to right relationship with the Creator of the universe.

Paul, in his first letter to the church in Thessolonica, prays that the God of peace would make sound the spirit, body, and soul of his brothers and sisters, so that they may be spotless at the second coming of the Lord Jesus Christ. This peace that our Lord brought down to earth that Christmas night was also the peace of a restored relationship between the Creator and His beloved Children.

The major reason for such deep and widespread unrest in the world was the lack of unity between people and God. Sin had dominion, and God was unreachable. The Prince of peace came to crash the rule of sin and create a whole and harmonious relationship between God and humankind. Praise the Lord that we are now able to be entirely made holy before the Lord of the universe giving us direct access to the throne of God. This is peace. This "wholeness" is shalom, and our hearts have been created with a deep and unending longing for the perfect union with our Creator. This is why Jesus came.

Reflect

Are there areas of brokenness and sin in your life that are currently causing a separation between yourself and God? What steps do you need to take to begin to restore your relationship with the Creator of the universe? Spend some time praying for God to break into those areas of your life so that your relationship may be restored, bringing the peace that comes only from the One we call "the Prince of Peace."

THURSDAY

Just a Little Peace and Quiet?

Read

"In that region there were shepherds living in the fields, keeping watch over their flock by night. Then an angel of the Lord stood before them, and the glory of the Lord shone around them, and they were terrified. But the angel said to them, "Do not be afraid; for see—I am bringing you good news of great joy for all the people: to you is born this day in the city of David a Savior, who is the Messiah, the Lord. This will be a sign for you: you will find a child wrapped in bands of cloth and lying in a manger." And suddenly there was with the angel a multitude of the heavenly host, praising God and saying, "Glory to God in the highest heaven, and on earth peace among those whom he favors!"

Luke 2:8-14

Who among us is not familiar with the pairing of the words peace and quiet? What parent has not longed for a moment of peace? When we as parents of young children, or school teachers, or nursery workers think of peace, we may think of some hard-won silence or maybe a few hours to close our eyes and rest. Maybe just a few seconds to simply hear ourselves think, or enjoy a few sips of coffee.

While one definition of peace is actual serenity, peace means so much more than quiet moments for which many of us long in the middle of our chaotic day.

Imagine the shepherds, resting with their sheep. They are enjoying some quiet time, probably dozing off, their heads bobbing with the heaviness of slumber, listening to the peaceful sounds of night. It is dark, not too much stimulation. The sheep aren't being too disruptive or wandering off. The stars are twinkling subtilely in the sky, not too bright, but just enough to provide a gentle natural night-light. The scene is serene, idyllic.

One minute, the shepherds are dozing. The next, the weight of slumber flees as they shield their eyes against what at first brush seems like the blazing sun greeting them and demolishing the darkness of night. As they squint, they see the outline of a massive figure, in the shape of the most resplendent soldier they have ever seen. Then the giant-soldier-sun-like-thing starts talking. Imagine the booming voice, shaking the ground like the explosive thunder of a lightning bolt that strikes two yards away. Blood drains from every face, shepherd and sheep alike. With the quaking ground and booming sound waves, everyone falls to their knees. What is that the shiny man is saying? Good news? Of great joy? A Messiah? In a manger?

What happens next is the polar opposite of peace in the form of serenity. Imagine how the flocks of sheep respond to the disruptive appearance of heavenly hosts. We're talking bright, shiny, loud heavenly armies crashing this restful sheep nap time party. Luke makes it clear that the shepherds were terrified, frozen in fear. Imagine dozens of sheep bleating in response to this appearance. No more subtle, twinkling stars. The sky is brighter than high noon now. No one will be able to sleep for months after this terrifying event. Not peaceful. Not one bit.

> This peace that the Messiah brings is the peace that pierces the darkness

Suddenly, the bleating of the sheep is overtaken by the sound of this heavenly army bursting into chorus:

"Glory to God in the highest heaven, and on earth peace among those whom he favors!"

This is peace? It is certainly not the "silent night" kind of peace. All is bright. It's blinding. But it is certainly not calm. This peace that the Messiah brings is the peace the pierces the darkness. It is the peace that restores wholeness and healing. It is the peace that reconciles opposing forces and brings us into right relationship with the King of the universe.

The "quiet" of the shepherd's night is replaced with the "peace" brought by the upside-down kingdom of heaven. This kind of peace would turn everyone's world upside down in the most amazing way imaginable.

Reflect

Spend some time imagining the scene as described above and place yourself in the shepherds shoes. What would you be thinking and feeling in a moment like this? What would it look like for peace to pierce through the broken and dark places in your life?

FRIDAY

Peace Before and Behind

Read

> *"I have said these things to you while I am still with you. But the Advocate, the Holy Spirit, whom the Father will send in my name, will teach you everything, and remind you of all that I have said to you. Peace I leave with you; my peace I give to you. I do not give to you as the world gives. Do not let your hearts be troubled, and do not let them be afraid."*
>
> *John 14:25-27*

When He came into the world, He was heralded as the "Prince of Peace." Peace, true peace, entered the world through the Christ child. He presented the reality of reconciliation between God and man. He laid the foundation for the rule of peace that will be actualized at His second coming. Peace was His means and His ends.

His very nature was peace, and He embodied peace. He brought a piercing peace, one that was disruptive of the disordered order of the broken universe, one that shattered the status quo and dumped the oppressors off of their soft, plush sofas. His peace brought discomfort and friction to those who benefited from the lack of peace.

This Savior, who brought peace, began the process of transforming hearts, thoughts, and souls so that we could become who we were created to be all along: beloved children in an intimate love-relationship with our Creator- Parent God.

And this Savior, the Prince of Peace, left us with a deposit of a new peace. This Advocate, the Spirit, is our deposit of Peace, the One who reminds us of the peace that rules in heaven and one day will rule on earth. This peace is the shalom that offers to rule our hearts and minds if we submit to the Lordship of God in our lives.

The peace that paved the way for the coming of the Christ child is the same peace that entered the hearts of the expectant members of the early church that fiery Sunday in the upper room.

The Holy Spirit, dwelling among us and within us, is our deposit of peace as we live in the already-but-not-yet kingdom of our Lord. The Holy Spirit is the One that can allow peace to rule our hearts and minds in a world that is still broken and shattered. Let us never push aside the peace that Christ ushered into this world and left as a deposit until His second coming, the peace that holds us together, making us whole.

Reflect

We are given the peace of Christ in our lives. What would it look like for you claim and embody this peace in your life? How might you invite the Holy Spirit into your heart and mind in deeper ways in order to come to a deeper understanding of the peace of God in your life?

SATURDAY

Blessed Are the Peacemakers

Read

"This is the testimony given by John when the Jews sent priests and Levites from Jerusalem to ask him, "Who are you?" He confessed and did not deny it, but confessed, "I am not the Messiah." And they asked him, "What then? Are you Elijah?" He said, "I am not." "Are you the prophet?" He answered, "No." Then they said to him, "Who are you? Let us have an answer for those who sent us. What do you say about yourself?" He said, "I am the voice of one crying out in the wilderness, 'Make straight the way of the Lord,'" as the prophet Isaiah said. Now they had been sent from the Pharisees. They asked him, "Why then are you baptizing if you are neither the Messiah, nor Elijah, nor the prophet?" John answered them, "I baptize with water. Among you stands one whom you do

*not know, the one who is coming after me;
I am not worthy to untie the thong of his
sandal." This took place in Bethany across
the Jordan where John was baptizing."*
John 1:19-28

John the Baptizer, the cousin of Jesus, in the core of his self-identity, existed only in the context of his relationship with Jesus Christ. When asked who he was, his first answer was in the negative highlighting who he was not: he was not Jesus Christ. He was not the star of the show, nor did he have any plans to be. He was not God. In his humility and his correct orientation with the Savior, he was secure in his identity.

The priests and Levites needed an answer for the church leaders who sent them to John, and he spoke of himself as merely a voice; one that declared the coming of the Lord and urgently begged listeners to make straight the way for the Lord; a voice pleading for peace, begging for hearts to bend to the coming King.

When we hear of other members of Jesus' family during His lifetime and ministry, we find a bunch of individuals who don't really take Him too seriously. We even hear Jesus say that a "prophet is not accepted in his hometown" (Luke 4:24). Yet, this cousin of Jesus, this peacemaker, takes Jesus seriously enough to lay down his own life. Ultimately for the sake of Christ, John will be beheaded (Mark 6:14-29).

John the Baptist, the peacemaker, makes way for peace in Bethany, baptizing across the Jordan. John the Baptist was the unborn child who leapt in Elizabeth's womb, when in the presence of the unborn Christ. This resonance of peace between the Savior and His cousin John the Baptizer would begin to clear the path for Jesus' march to the cross where ultimate peace would be achieved. The martyrdom of John, the cousin of Jesus, foreshadowed the crucifixion of Christ, and the greatest Peacemaker would win eternal reconciliation for all children of God.

Blessed are the peacemakers, for theirs is the kingdom of heaven.

Reflect

Following the example of John the Baptist, how does your life point to Jesus? How might God be calling you to be a voice that points others to Christ? What ways can you extend peace to others in order to point them to the giver of peace, Jesus?

LOVE

WEEK 4

"This new force—perfect, healing, redeeming love—begins its work through the ministry of one man."

MONDAY

What if...

Read

> *"There is no fear in love, but perfect love casts out fear; for fear has to do with punishment, and whoever fears has not reached perfection in love. We love because he first loved us."*
>
> 1 John 4:18-19

Why is love the final gift of Advent? What is this climax that we have been building for during the previous three weeks? We have traversed our deepest brokenness, hurts, and needs and found peace, hope, and joy. And this journey through our need to the Giver of all perfect gifts, the greatest Gift Himself, leads us to the candle of love.

Ann Voskamp, in One Thousands Gifts, her journey into gratitude, states emphatically, "All fear is but the notion that God's love ends."[1] John tells us that "perfect love drives out fear, because there is no fear in love." What is it about love that cripples fear in the life of a believer? On the flip side, what is it about fear that calls to question the integrity of God's love for us?

Here we all are hanging on with all of our might on this moving globe- this ball of oxygen, silicon, iron, calcium, sodium, potassium, and magnesium, hanging precariously in a delicate balance, and every one of the approximately 7.5 billion members of the human race is familiar with fear. And do you know what else? Every single one of all 7.5 billion of our hearts is beating desperately for the sake of love. And what if dear Ann Voskamp's statement is true? Let's state it again and sit with it; let it sink into the marrow of our bones: "All fear is but the notion that God's love ends."

What if this last week of Advent is the key that unlocks the door to our safety? What if we can enter into this final week of Advent with the knowledge that God's love, indeed, is interminable? It will not, cannot, ever, through the span of eternity, ever end.

How do we know this? Jesus Christ, God incarnate, stripped Himself of His God-status, squeezed into human skin, stepped out of Kai-

---

1   Voskamp, Ann. *One Thousand Gifts* (Eugene, Oregon: Zondervan) Page 161.

ros (God's) time into Chronos (human) time and demonstrated the never-ending, unshakable, unchanging, always and forever love of God.

What if we really, deep down in the most remote chambers of our souls, embraced this truth? What if we really knew how deeply and overwhelmingly loved we really are? I believe that if we could truly "live loved", our fears would be assuaged, and our lives would begin to beat the heart of Christ into the world.

Reflect

Are there areas in your life where fear is preventing you from truly living? What would it look like for you to allow love from both God and others to speak life and freedom into your life? How might you live differently if you fully embraced the truth that God's love for you is never-ending, unshakable, unchanging always and forever?

TUESDAY

The Love Story

Read

"So God created humankind in his image, in the image of God he created them; male and female he created them."

Genesis 1:27

"In the beginning was the Word, and the Word was with God, and the Word was God. He was in the beginning with God. All things came into being through him, and without him not one thing came into being. What has come into being in him was life, and the life was the light of all people. The light shines in the darkness, and the darkness did not overcome it...And the Word became flesh and lived among us, and we have seen his glory, the glory as of a father's only son, full of grace and truth."

John 1:1-5; 14

God, in Trinitarian form, existed, one, together, from the beginning, when They began to speak to life the love story of creation. When They created humanity and spoke that we were good. When God, with the Word, Jesus Christ, spoke us into existence, declaring us His people, made in His very own image. This love story, which began with "once upon a time," or "in the beginning."

John 1 echoes Genesis 1 with overwhelming clarity, as we see deeper into the creation scene, where Father and Son breathed life and spoke life together into a people that they created with love.

If all of fear is but the belief that love does not exist, with the intimate love story presented in creation, how could we ever be afraid?

God, in His foreknowledge, with His first breath of life into humanity's lungs, knows what sacrifice will have to be made in order to restore the love relationship between Creator and created. Yet still He breathes that first life. The Son, in relationship with the Father, from the beginning knows that He will ultimately die on that earth that they are creating for the sake of humanity, and still He declares the goodness of His creation, man and woman.

God's love is the most consistent, most powerful force in the universe. It is what knits the story of humanity together. God's love is what draws the Old Testament and New Testament to the central focus of the Cross of Christ.

Love, the strongest force in the universe, the gravity that holds our feet to the foundation of grace, is embodied in the Alpha and Omega, in "I Am who I Am" who Moses met in the wilderness, in the one that John the Baptizer heralded as "the one coming after me; I am not worthy to untie the thong of his sandal" (John 1:27). This sandal-clad foot to which John referred was the divine foot that touched the profane sand of this filthy planet in order to make manifest His love for you and me.

This love that is so real, not even we can prevent it from breaking through our mess of sin and disobedience. This love shoved through our resistance, trampled over death, and declared the final destruction of all fear. The love that said, "No force on earth or under the earth can cause me to retreat." This is the Love that we celebrate this final week of Advent.

This is the love that created us, and the love that sustains us.

Reflect

Reflect on the idea that God's love for you has no bounds. It existed before you were born and nothing you do can separate you from that love. What would it look like for God's love to break through the brokenness and mess of your life to knit you back together? To remove all fear and fill you with His perfect love?

WEDNESDAY

He Shall Reign Forever and Ever

Read

"When the oppressor is no more, and de-struction has ceased, and marauders have vanished from the land, then a throne shall be established in steadfast love in the tent of David, and on it shall sit in faithfulness a ruler who seeks justice and is swift to do what is right."

Isaiah 16:4b-5

Isaiah is speaking to Israel, who is under the tyrannical reign of the Moabites. The nation of Moab is described as proud, arrogant, and inso-lent (verse 6). They are liars (verse 7).

Israel is steeped in grief, wailing, heartbroken, and bone-tired. Their dream of freedom and abundance is shattered, and they are hollow with fear.

How many of us today are bone-tired, weary, and undone? How many, like Israel, feel withered, longing for abundance and rest, but hard-pressed to find a vision of hope even in your deepest imagination?

We could be drowning in debt, or facing abuse or the aftermath of abuse. We could be facing a laundry list of medical diagnoses, or one that places our expiration date much sooner than we ever anticipated. We could be walking beside a loved one through chronic or terminal illness, or navigating what seems like a dead-end relationship. We could be trying to hold onto sanity and hope in the midst of blinding and derailing mental illness that causes us to question everything that we have ever believed to be reality. Bondage, pain, and suffering come in as many forms as there are people on the face of the planet. Many of us stand in solidarity with our brothers and sisters under the thumb of the kingdom of Moab.

Isaiah breaks through with a ray of hope, one that breaks the rule of fear and darkness. This promise:

"When the oppressors will be no more..." There will actually be a day when the oppressors will be gone. Is that even possible?

"A throne shall be established in steadfast love..." Does anyone actually rule out of steadfast love? Are you telling me that someone would use something other than fear to rule over us? That there is a chance that we will no longer be puppets, controlled and manipulated to act in a way that only advances the schemes of the one in charge? Someone will care for us who will possibly have our best interest at heart?

"And on it shall sit in faithfulness…." A faithful ruler? What does that mean? Someone who stands on truth, who speaks a language other than the language of lies? Someone whom we can trust; whom we can let our guards down with? Who will actually rule in honesty?

"A ruler who seeks justice and is swift to do what is right…" This ruler could possibly be one who does not capitalize on the weakness of the poor? This ruler would punish the evil and care for the downcast and the underdog? This ruler would not be bought with money or swayed by his own power? This King would not allow injustice to rule but would make all the wrong things right? We could live an existence where we no longer have to throw up our hands in exasperation as the persecutors go unquestioned and weak suffer even more?

We have been longing for freedom. We have been living in fear. We have fallen for lesser loves, ones that run out, that eventually end. We have been ruled by oppressors, and we long for a benevolent, just, and righteous King who rules on the foundation of steadfast love. We have been desperate to trust in a love that doesn't threaten to pull the rug out from under our feet.

The One for whom we have been longing has arrived! Isaiah prophesied of His coming, and his foretelling of this King gave the Hebrew nation hope. We have the record of His arrival and victory, and the promise of His reign to come. This knowledge causes our fears to crumble. This love that has come and is coming to make right all wrongs will never end.

The one for whom we have been longing has arrived!

The reign of the oppressors has expired. It has lived its life, had a heyday, and the sun is setting on its kingdom.

Handel's Hallelujah Chorus gives us a glimpse into the celebration of the Lordship of Jesus Christ and the kingdom of heaven: "The kingdom of this world has become the kingdom of our Lord and of His Christ, and He shall reign forever and ever" (1741). Imagine 7.5 billion voices singing this resounding chorus together as we praise the world's most faithful Ruler in history.

Our fear crumbles when we finally acknowledge that our Lord, who shall reign forever and ever, is the embodiment of the loving-kindness for which our souls have been yearning.

Reflect

Have you ever experienced times in your life where you have felt weary and undone? Are there areas in your life where you are longing for rest and even abundance?

THURSDAY

Extravagant Love

Read

"He whom God has sent speaks the words of God, for he gives the Spirit without measure. The Father loves the Son and has placed all things in his hands. Whoever believes in the Son has eternal life; whoever disobeys the Son will not see life, but must endure God's wrath."

John 3:34-36

"As the Father has loved me, so I have loved you; abide in my love."

John 15:9

The love relationship of the Holy Trinity is the prototype of love relationships. Before any other relationship existed, the Trinity existed in perfect love. The Father, Son, and Spirit love because they embody love. God is love because God's trinitarian identity is one of perfect love.

The Father loves the Son. Jesus' primary identity on earth was the Son, the one whom the Father loves. John identified himself as the disciple that Jesus loves. Could it be that John witnessed the love-relationship of two parties of the Trinity and discovered that the perfect love existent in the Trinity emanated from the incarnated second person of the trinity? Could it be that John, as he saw the love relationship between the Father and Son, also experienced the waves of perfect love from Jesus in their day-to-day relationship. If this perfect love, created in the Trinity, poured out of Jesus Christ into each of His relationships, how could each disciple not identify himself as the "one Jesus loved?"

Why do we learn so much about love through the gospel of John and in the other books penned by John the disciple of Jesus? I believe that John had an astute perception of the love of Christ, maybe because of his personality, maybe because of his unique vantage point, probably from a combination of factors. Whatever the reason, John's perspective is infinitely valuable in grasping the love of Jesus Christ.

I wonder how John's sense of self changed as he slowly absorbed his new identity as the "disciple that Jesus loved?" I imagine that he stood a little taller, that he saw the world with a greater clarity and that his areas of brokenness morphed and mended in light of the love that flooded his life.

I also imagine that in his secure identity as the beloved of Christ he was set free to love others more fully, and to pour love out like a drink offering, just as his Savior poured love out to him. The remarkable thing about living loved is that we tend to love others more fully and profoundly. Experiencing perfect love produces the fruit of perfect love in our lives, which is more love, which has an exponential cascade effect on all those around us. (Imagine a pay-it-forward line in Starbucks, but a trillion times better).

Jesus lived in the Godhead trinitarian relationship of perfect, complete love. In His state of perfect, complete love, He self-emptied and descended onto this spinning ball of brokenness, pouring rivers of love in every direction. Some received it, and some did not recognize it. Remember, "The light shines in the darkness, but the darkness has not yet perceived it" (John 1:5). To those who did recognize it and receive the Love, they were crowned with the title of "God's beloved" and they too poured out love like streams into a parched wasteland.

That is how perfect love works: love produces love, which gives more love. Love grows, like an ocean that pours into streams, and branches into lakes, and waters the thirsty ground which never knew it needed love until it tastes it for the first time.

A people who had no idea how much fear they lived in discover that perfect love has sent their fear running for the hills. As a result, they pour forth love like rivers rolling down the mountain- side, delighting in going lower and lower as their love waters the thirsty lands.

Reflect

Have you ever thought about the love that existed in the trinity before time?   Have you ever felt the love of God wash over you in such a way that you were able to compre-hend the love of God in a deeper way? How can God's love for you help you to pour forth love to others? Have you ever experienced love producing more love in your life and relationships?

FRIDAY

The Giver of All Good Gifts

Read

"Every generous act of giving, with every perfect gift, is from above, coming down from the Father of lights, with whom there is no variation or shadow due to change. In fulfillment of his own purpose he gave us birth by the word of truth, so that we would become a kind of first fruits of his creatures."
James 1:17-18

"For a child has been born for us, a son given to us; authority rests upon his shoulders; and he is named Wonderful Counselor, Mighty God, Everlasting Father, Prince of Peace."
Isaiah 9:6

"Therefore, since we are justified by faith, we have peace with God through our Lord Jesus

Christ; Therefore just as one man's trespass led to condemnation for all, so one man's act of righteousness leads to justification and life for all."

Romans 5:1; 18

There is a moment in history, the moment when that baby opens his divinely human eyes for a first blurry look around the stable, where evil stops in its tracks recognizing that its conqueror has breathed His first breath. The forces of Hell tremble around the circumference of the globe, and the forces of righteousness swell with anticipation triggered by the stirrings of the mighty winds of heaven.

There is a moment when in His kindness, goodness, sovereignty, and love God graces earth with the greatest gift that she never even knew she needed. Until one-by-one, the honest, with open and contrite hearts, lay eyes on Jesus Christ. Then, one-by-one, the human race begins to realize that a new force has been released into the atmosphere of our tattered, tired, derailed planet. This new force—perfect, healing, redeeming love—begins its gradual work through the ministry of one man.

What is on your list of gifts this Christmas? What have you requested? What have you purchased or made? How deeply have you invested yourself in coming up with the "perfect gift?" Why do we so often feel like finding the perfect present is a losing battle?

In the context of our culture of excess, we often have to search and search for something, anything, that our loved ones might not already have. What do you get for someone who has it all? How many parents struggle with coming up with gifts for children who seem to have flooded their rooms, toy rooms, living rooms, storage rooms, and garages with more toys than any one child could ever play with? And still we try, often to no avail, to find the "perfect gifts" for our loved ones at Christmas time. We bang our heads repeatedly against the proverbial wall of consumerism and marketing, feeling the pressure to make Christmas "extra special" for our family.

And then there is God, the Giver of good gifts, as described by James the brother of Jesus. James, the kid that grew up alongside Jesus, who probably dug in the dirt with him, may have wrestled and learned to read and write with Jesus as a youth and adolescent, and matured to know Jesus in His short earthly ministry. James, whose very brother was the greatest gift that God could give, who gave the greatest gift that humanity could ever dream: right standing with God and eternal, abundant life in the present world and the world to come. James knew personally the giver of the greatest gift in the world. Thus, we should listen to his words.

We give gifts as echoes of the gift of the Christ child at Christmas. Yet somewhere along the way, we forgot that the greatest gift has already been given to

> We give gifts as echoes of the gift of the Christ Child at Christmas.

us. Have we embraced the love-gift of the Father God to us, His beloved sons and daughters?

Do we give out of a frantic, frenzied compulsion to "make Christmas special," or do we give out of the overflow of the love that Christ has poured into our hearts through His ultimate gift of love on the cross?

Do we, secure in our identities and at peace with God through Jesus Christ, pour into the lives of others that same grace, love, and peace? We know that we have nothing to prove, nothing to earn, and nothing to manufacture. We are loved, period. We can lean into the gift of love given by Christ, and soak up His affection for us. Rest in His loving kindness long enough and you will find that you start to exhibit interesting behavior. You start loving like Him. You start pouring out what is being poured into you. As your cup is filled by the Giver of all good gifts, you, in turn, become a giver of gifts. As God pours His love into our hearts, our hearts start to pour out love, joy, peace, patience, kindness, goodness, and faithfulness (Galatians 5:22-23). These are the gifts that really count. These are the gifts that God, in His love, has for us who will open our hands to receive.

Reflect

Have you ever struggled to come up with the perfect gift for someone? Has anyone ever gotten you the perfect gift? What would it look like for you to begin giving out of the overflow of the love which Christ first gave to us?

SATURDAY

No Longer Condemned

Read

"For God so loved the world that he gave his only Son, so that everyone who believes in him may not perish but may have eternal life. Indeed, God did not send the Son into the world to condemn the world, but in order that the world might be saved through him."

John 3:16-17

Do we think that God sent His son to condemn? Deep down, do we believe that He came to this planet to tally up a score, to come down and monitor us? Like a spy sent over enemy lines, to gather data and report back to the great scorekeeper in heaven, as if we were being reported on? Graded? To see if we measure up to the expectations and standards? To see if our sacrifices are complete and thorough? To investigate our actions, motives, even our dreams? To decide if we are more good or more evil? To be like some kind of cosmic Santa, making the final decision about whether we have been "naughty" or "nice?" The stakes are much higher than a piece of coal in our stockings, aren't they? We are talking eternity.

How many of us still hold onto a piece, or even a sliver, of this distorted perspective? That Jesus came to judge the world?

Following arguably the most famous, frequently quoted verse in the Bible, John 3:16, we stumble upon a declaration of God's true purpose in sending His son: "For God sent His son not to condemn the world, but that the world might be saved by Him." Isaiah, when referring prophetically to Christ, states, "A bruised reed He will not break" (Isaiah 42:3). Also, referring to Jesus, Isaiah says in chapter 40, verse 11, "He shall feed His flock like a shepherd: He shall gather the lambs in his arms and carry them in his bosom." Psalm 147:3, "He heals the broken-hearted and binds up their wounds."

Do you get the picture? Does this sound like a secret spy, sent to gather intel on a rotten group of hopeless, corrupt people? Does this sound like a description of one who came to judge and condemn? Not from what I gather. I see a loving Father, compassionately sending a self-denying Son, not only to save the world, but to die for the world. "Greater love has no one than this, than to lay down one's life for one's friends"(John 15:13). Not only does He lay down His life for us in love, but he calls us friends.

"This is love, not that we loved Him, but that He loved us and laid down His life for us" (1 John 4:10, paraphrased). We could pour out verses about God's love for us all day, and we would still have plenty of material to work with.

God loves us, so...Jesus.

Jesus, the Word was with God in the beginning, when God breathed life into His creation.

Jesus, the sacrificial lamb, who came into the world in love, through love, for love, all for us. To restore us to right relationship with God.

Jesus, from the lineage of Jesse, the father of David, through the family line of a hodgepodge group of harlots and ruffians. An unlikely group of players through whom God chose to pour life back into an emaciated, broken world.

Jesus, the one who brought joy and laughter into the world even while in the womb of Mary, as she encountered Elizabeth and the unborn John the Baptist.

Jesus, the complexity of all-God and all-human, who, all for the love of you and of me, descended and made Himself nothing, being obedient to death on the cross, becoming the lowest of the low, so that we may be lifted up to life in our fellowship with Him in His death.

Jesus, who paved a new road, a way in the desert, one of submission, humility, and servant-leadership, who taught us to wash one another's feet, and literally give our very lives for one another.

Jesus, the King of kings and Lord of lords, who in neonatal state, rested in the very trough that animals ate from.

This Jesus did not come to condemn. He did not come to heap on shame, but to lift up the wounded, bruised, and desperate. He came to pour love into a love-hungry planet. He came to present a new way of the cross, the way of peace, hope and joy, through the world-transforming power of perfect love.

God did not send Jesus to judge us; Jesus came to rescue us. Don't run from the Christ child. He is your one and only life-line, and the most perfect gift that God could ever give you. We have never wanted and needed anything more than we need Him now.

Reflect

What distortions have you held about God that are counter to His nature of love? How would the way you live look different if you embraced the truth of God's deep love for you? Are there areas of your life where you need Jesus to rescue you? Invite Him in. Invite the Spirit to pour out this amazing love into your heart and mind.

APPENDIX

SMALL GROUP RESOURCES

SESSION 1

GOD OF HOPE

The world and our lives are filled with the mark of unmet expectations as our hopes, dreams and desires go unfulfilled. At times the weight of these can lead us into despair and hopelessness. But our God is a God of hope. God is one who, no matter the depths of our despair, extends grace and hope in Jesus.

Prayer: Have a member of the group open up in prayer asking the Holy Spirit to open your hearts and minds to the ways God desires to speak to each person through this session.

Read

Read the passage several times through slowly and prayerfully. If in an appropriate setting, you can have someone read it once out loud so others can listen to it. As you read, what phrase, word or image from the text resonates, stands out or connects with you? What is something that raises questions for you?

Luke 1:5-25

5 In the days of King Herod of Judea, there was a priest named Zechariah, who belonged to the priestly order of Abijah. His wife was a descendant of Aaron, and her name was Elizabeth. 6 Both of them were righteous before God, living blamelessly according to all the commandments and regulations of the Lord. 7 But they had no children, because Elizabeth was barren, and both were getting on in years. 8 Once when he was serving as priest before God and his section was on duty, 9 he was chosen by lot, according to the custom of the priesthood, to enter the sanctuary of the Lord and offer incense. 10 Now at the time of the incense offering, the whole assembly of the people was praying outside. 11 Then there appeared to him an angel of the Lord, standing at the right side of the altar of incense. 12 When Zechariah saw him, he was terrified; and fear overwhelmed him. 13 But the angel said to him, "Do not be afraid, Zechariah, for your prayer has been heard. Your wife Elizabeth will bear you a son, and you will name him John. 14 You will have joy and gladness, and many will rejoice at his birth, 15 for he will be great in the sight of the Lord. He must never drink wine or strong drink; even before his birth he will be filled with the Holy Spirit. 16 He will turn many of the people of Israel to the Lord their God. 17 With the spirit and power of Elijah he will go before him, to turn the hearts of parents to their children, and the disobedient to the wisdom of the righteous, to make ready a people prepared for the Lord." 18 Zechariah said to the angel, "How will I know that this is so? For I am an old man, and my wife is getting on in years." 19 The angel replied, "I am Gabriel. I stand in the presence of God, and I have been sent to speak to you and to bring you this good news. 20 But now, because you did not believe my words, which will be fulfilled in their time, you will become mute, unable to speak, until the day these things occur." 21 Meanwhile the people were waiting for Zechariah, and wondered at his delay in the sanctuary. 22 When he did come out, he could not speak to them, and they realized that he had seen a vision in the sanctuary. He kept motioning to them and remained unable to speak. 23 When his time of service was ended, he went to his home. 24 After those days his wife Elizabeth conceived, and for five months she remained in seclusion. She said, 25 "This is what the Lord has done for me when he looked favorably on me and took away the disgrace I have endured among my people."

Setting the Scene

- **In the time of Zechariah and Elizabeth it was often assumed that being childless was a punishment for sinful living. Because of this, being childless would not only bring heartache, but also often social alienation from others along with no one to care for you in your old age.[1]**
- **Entering into the temple of the Lord was often a once in a lifetime event for a priest. This would have been a very special occasion for Zechariah.**

[1] Keener, Craig. IVP Bible Background Commentary: New Testament. 1993.

Reflect

After reading the passage several times through, spend some time discussing the passage with those you are gathered with. What stood out or connected with you? What insights did you get from the passage? What questions were brought up for you? Listen carefully to one another, allowing everyone the chance to share as you reflect on the passage together.

Other questions you might like to explore:

1. The reading said Elizabeth and Zechariah were aging, possibly much past what would be considered child-bearing age. How much hope do you think they had left?

2. Zechariah responded to the news of joy and hope from the angel with doubt (vs.18). Why was it so hard for Zechariah to see hope after such a powerful experience?

3. God moved in their lives in a significant way to bring hope, not only to them but to many others. Have you ever experienced God move in significant ways in your own life that gave you and perhaps others hope?

Respond

Challenge ideas:

1. **Reflect on different time(s) in your life when God has breathed hope into your life. Is there someone in your life who needs to hear this story of hope? Ask the Holy Spirit to speak in and through you and share the hope you have experienced in Christ with someone this week.**

2. **Spend some time this week through prayer and journaling voicing any disappointments you have with God. Ask the Holy Spirit to breathe life and hope into your life once again. Also share these with a friend you can trust asking them to pray for you. Who knows - God may even use them to speak hope into your life.**

3. **Other ideas? Is there an idea your small group might like to act on together that came out of your time together? Go act on it!**

Prayer:

As you close out your time together, spend some time praying for one another sharing any special prayer requests anyone in the group might have. Also spend some time praying that the Holy Spirit would breathe life and hope into each of your lives this week and beyond.

SESSION 2

GOD OF JOY

Let's face it: There are simply times in our lives when we don't feel much joy. The shadows of sadness in our lives seems to cover up the light of joy. Even when we feel like we are walking in the darkness we can have confidence that there is a light on the horizon. When we see this great light, the light of Christ, it brings joy. Because our God is a God of joy!

Prayer: Have a member of the group open up in prayer asking the Holy Spirit to open your hearts and minds to the ways God desires to speak to each person through this session.

Read

Read the passage several times through slowly and prayerfully. If in an appropriate setting, you can have someone read it once out loud so others can listen to it. As you read, what phrase, word or image from the text resonates, stands out or connects with you? What is something that raises questions for you?

Luke 1:39-56

And Mary said, "My soul magnifies the Lord, 47 and my spirit rejoices in God my Savior, 48 for he has looked with favor on the lowliness of his servant. Surely, from now on all generations will call me blessed; 49 for the Mighty One has done great things for me, and holy is his name. 50 His mercy is for those who fear him from generation to generation. 51 He has shown strength with his arm; he has scattered the proud in the thoughts of their hearts. 52 He has brought down the powerful from their thrones, and lifted up the lowly; 53 he has filled the hungry with good things, and sent the rich away empty. 54 He has helped his servant Israel, in remembrance of his mercy, 55 according to the promise he made to our ancestors, to Abraham and to his descendants forever." 56 And Mary remained with her about three months and then returned to her home.

Setting the Scene

- Mary had just received the news that she was pregnant. What normally would have brought great joy instead brought fear and trepidation for Mary.
- Mary was unmarried and a virgin. This news could have led to Joseph dismissing or divorcing her, ruining any future plans for her life she might have had.
- This text is often entitled "Mary's song of Joy" or praise.

Reflect

After reading the passage several times through, spend some time discussing the passage with those who are gathered around you. What stood out or connected with you? What insights did you get from the passage? What questions were brought up for you? Listen carefully to one another, allowing everyone the chance to share as you reflect on the passage together.

Other questions you might like to explore:

1.   **Have you ever experienced joy in the midst of a situation that would not normally bring joy? What was that like?**

2.   **Mary was rejoicing in the midst of what some might say was suffering. Why do you think Mary responded this way?**

3.   **Have you ever witnessed in your own life or in someone else's life a great amount of joy in the midst of a situation that would seemingly call for another response?**

Respond

Challenge ideas:

1.   **Is there a situation in your life right now through which you are struggling to find joy? Spend**

some time reflecting on areas of your life where you can find place for joy and thank God as Mary did for giving you space to experience that joy.

2.   Perhaps you are in a season of life that is filled with joy. If that is you, how might God be calling you to share that joy with others as Mary did with Elizabeth? Find one or more people to intentionally share your joy with. We may find that it can be infectious.

3.   Other ideas? Is there an idea your small group might like to act on together that came out of your time together? Go act on it!

Prayer:

As you close out your time together, spend some time praying for one another and any special prayer requests anyone in the group might have. Also spend some time praying that the Holy Spirit would breathe life and joy into each of your lives this week and beyond.

SESSION 3

GOD OF PEACE

As the people of God, we often live in a constant state of stress or anxiety as Christmas draws near and we are rushing around to get everything ready. I often wonder in these times, where is the peace? We are longing for something more, but we can't quite place our finger on it. Possibly because though we were created for it, we have never truly experienced the object of this obscure longing. We look around and we see oppression and injustice at every turn and we cry out asking "when will it end?" Deep down we all long for the day where there is true peace. What if true peace comes not in the way we expect it; what if it comes in the small, unassuming form of a little baby named Jesus? When we submit to this Jesus, offering our very hearts and minds to the Creator of the universe, the Spirit of God will begin to breathe new life and peace into our lives.

Prayer: Have a member of the group open up in prayer asking the Holy Spirit to open your hearts and minds to the ways God desires to speak to each person through this session.

Read

Read the passage several times through slowly and prayerfully. If in an appropriate setting, you can have someone read it once out loud so others can listen to it. As you read, what phrase, word or image from the text resonates, stands out or connects with you? What is something that raises questions for you?

Matthew 2:16-18

"When Herod saw that he had been tricked by the wise men, he was infuriated, and he sent and killed all the children in and around Bethlehem who were two years old or under, according to the time that he had learned from the wise men. 17 Then was fulfilled what had been spoken through the prophet Jeremiah:

18 "A voice was heard in Ramah, wailing and loud lamentation, Rachel weeping for her children; she refused to be consoled, because they are no more."

Setting the Scene

- When King Herod heard of Jesus' birth he was greatly troubled because he saw it as a threat to his reign. So he tried to use the wise men to figure out Jesus' location.
- When the wise men caught on to the fact that Herod was using them, and had ill intent for Jesus, they returned a different way to avoid Herod.

> • Every major route home for the Wise Men would have taken them through Jerusalem right by King Herod. When they never passed back by, he would have known they were avoiding him and he became furious.[1]
>
> ---
>
> 1 Keener, Craig. IVP Bible Background Commentary: New Testament. 1993.

Reflect

After reading the passage several times through, spend some time discussing the passage with those you are gathered with. What stood out or connected with you? What insights did you get from the passage? What questions were brought up for you? Listen carefully to one another, allowing everyone the chance to share as you reflect on the passage together.

Other questions you might like to explore:

1.   There didn't seem to be much peace after the birth of the "Prince of Peace." Why would Herod react in this way?

2.   Herod seems to have reacted to what was supposed to be a positive event out of fear. Due to this, it brought sadness and even death instead of peace. Have you ever reacted to a positive situation out of fear (most likely not as extreme as Herod!) which in turn caused issues instead of peace?

3.   Have you seen or experienced others reacting

to something out of fear? Was this response helpful to the situation? If so, how? If not, why not?

4.   How might God want to bring peace in the midst of our seemingly hectic, stressful, and often conflict filled lives? What part is God calling us to play in bringing this peace?

Respond

Challenge ideas:

1.   Are there area(s) in your life where you have been operating out of fear? Spend some time this week writing out all of your fears. Then one by one invite the Holy Spirit to enter into your heart and mind to free you from those fears so you can be a person of peace.

2.   Are there individual(s) in your life with whom you are not at peace? Were there fears driving the discord in a relationship? Perhaps God might be calling you to reach out to them extending a hand of peace. Pray and invite the Holy Spirit to give you strength.

3.   Other ideas? Is there an idea your small group might like to act on together that came out of your time together? Go act on it!

Prayer:

As you close out your time together, spend some time praying for one another and any special prayer requests anyone in the group might have. Also spend some time praying that the Holy Spirit would breathe peace into each of your lives this week and beyond.

SESSION 4

GOD OF LOVE

We love because He first loved us. Our blueprint for love is written in the heart of that Child born in Bethlehem under the star that declared His presence to the world. Without that little heart beating its rhythm of love for the entire world, we would be bereft of love for one another. This is how we know what love is: Jesus Christ came into the world, to lay down His life for us. God the Father, from the beginning of time, is His omniscience, knew that His Son, the sacrificial lamb, must be slain for the sins of us, His beloved sons and daughters. Once we receive the love-gift of the Son's poured out blood we are free to love as He loves us.

Prayer: Have a member of the group open up in prayer asking the Holy Spirit to open your hearts and minds to the ways God desires to speak to each person through this session.

Read

Read the passage several times through slowly and prayerfully. If in an appropriate setting, you can have someone read it once out loud so others can listen to it. As you read, what phrase, word or image from the text resonates, stands out or connects with you? What is something that raises questions for you?

John 1:1-14

In the beginning was the Word, and the Word was with God, and the Word was God. 2 He was in the beginning with God. 3 All things came into being through him, and without him not one thing came into being. What has come into being 4 in him was life, and the life was the light of all people. 5 The light shines in the darkness, and the darkness did not overcome it. 6 There was a man sent from God, whose name was John. 7 He came as a witness to testify to the light, so that all might believe through him. 8 He himself was not the light, but he came to testify to the light. 9 The true light, which enlightens everyone, was coming into the world. 10 He was in the world, and the world came into being through him; yet the world did not know him. 11 He came to what was his own, and his own people did not accept him. 12 But to all who received him, who believed in his name, he gave power to become children of God, 13 who were born, not of blood or of the will of the flesh or of the will of man, but of God. 14 And the Word became flesh and lived among us, and we have seen his glory, the glory as of a father's only son, full of grace and truth.

Setting the Scene

• Part of Jewish tradition passed down was the idea that God's law was offered to every nation on Mount Sinai but only Israel at that time accepted it.[1] John in verse 9 is reinforcing the idea that God's covenant love is meant for all.

• In the opening chapters of John he is pointing back to the book of Genesis where we find God creating in the beginning. He is pointing to the Triune nature of God and that Jesus existed at the beginning of time.

1   Keener, Craig. IVP Bible Background Commentary: New Testament. 1993.

Reflect

After reading the passage several times through, spend some time discussing the passage with those you are gathered with. What stood out or connected with you? What insights did you get from the passage? What questions were brought up for you? Listen carefully to one another, allowing everyone the chance to share as you reflect on the passage together.

Other questions you might like to explore:

1.   Have you ever thought about the idea that Jesus existed when God created the world?

2.   What does it mean for Jesus to be the true light as John refers to in this passage? How does the idea that darkness cannot overcome light reveal the never-ending love of God?

3.   Have you ever thought of yourself as a child of God? Of God as a parent who deeply and unconditionally loves you?

4.   The scripture says the Word, Jesus, became flesh and dwelt among us. How does God's willingness to humble himself and dwell among us speak to the love of God in our lives?

Respond

Challenge ideas:

1.   Spend some time this week reflecting on the magnitude of God's love for you. What does it mean for you to live as a child of God? Is there someone in your life with whom you can share how much God loves them? Don't wait, share God's love with them this week.

2.   Are there areas of darkness in your life that you need to let God's light and love into? Spend some time this week confessing these things to God and also sharing them with someone you can confide in. Invite the Holy Spirit to breathe light and love into those areas of your life.

3.   Other ideas? Is there an idea your small group might like to act on together that came out of your time together? Go act on it!

Prayer:

As you close out your time together, spend some time praying for one another and any special prayer requests anyone in the group might have. Ask the Holy Spirit to open your hearts and minds to the unfathomable, overwhelming, matchless love of God. Pray that the members of your group might experience the love of God, so that you can go forth and love as Christ loved us and gave Himself for us.

About the Authors

Megan and Jordan currently live in Wichita, Kansas with two children Lily and Elijah, ages five and four. In addition to raising two preschoolers and multiple pets, this past year they launched a satellite campus of Aldersgate United Methodist Church called Renew where Jordan currently leads as campus pastor. Megan helps lead women's small groups and sings in worship. Megan has experienced many life-altering medical diagnoses over the past several years. As a result, Megan requires extra help and medical care to manage daily life. Life is definitely never dull, but they are grateful to be on this journey together as they seek to share the hope, joy, peace, love and healing of Jesus with all of those they encounter. They love Jesus with all of their hearts and in the midst of it all are grateful that Jesus is the light that illuminates our darkness.